Gardening Basics FOR DUMMIES®

POCKET EDITION

by Steven A. Frowine
with the Editors of the
National Gardening Association

Wiley Publishing, Inc.

Gardening Basics For Dummies® Pocket Edition

Published by
Wiley Publishing, Inc.
111 River St.
Hoboken, NJ 07030-5774
www.wiley.com

Published simultaneously in Canada

For general information on our other products and services, please contact our Customer Care Department within the U.S. at 877-762-2974, outside the U.S. at 317-572-3993, or fax 317-572-4002.

For technical support, please visit www.wiley.com/techsupport.

Wiley also publishes its books in a variety of electronic formats. Some content that appears in print may not be available in electronic books.

ISBN: 978-0-470-49968-9

Manufactured in the United States of America

10 9 8 7 6 5 4 3 2 1

Table of Contents

Introduction

Aren't you lucky! You are entering or are already part of the most popular and rewarding lifelong hobby that exists — worldwide. Gardening is a common language that knows no national, socioeconomic, or age boundaries. It's a common thread that binds all of us together. Gardeners have an instant bond, no matter what their level of experience.

Because gardening is a huge topic that encompasses a wide field of cultivation interests and disciplines, it's impossible for any one book to cover everything there is to know about gardening. However, when you're armed with the gardening basics, like those presented in this book, you're ready for just about anything that the art of gardening can throw at you.

Icons Used in This Book

Icons are the cute little pictures that show up in the margins of the book, right next to certain blocks of text. Here's what those icons stand for:

This image points out some ecological tips that you can follow and use to ensure that your gardening is truly Earth–friendly.

Gardeners sometimes speak their own lingo, which can be a bit confusing for people who are just getting their feet wet (or dirty) in the gardening process. This icon helps to identify and clarify the most common terms you encounter.

This icon points out some major ideas in the book — stuff well worth remembering.

The Tip icon flags notable gardening information that even experienced gardeners may not know. This info can save you time and frustration.

This icon alerts you to possible problems to watch out for or avoid. These problems may result in injury or, at the very least, a bad gardening experience.

Where to Go from Here

You've got your minibook copy of *Gardening Basics For Dummies* — now what? This minibook is a reference, so if you need information on annuals, head to Chapter 3. Or if you're interested in finding out about veggies, go straight to Chapter 5. Or heck, start with Chapter 1 and read the chapters in order . . . you rebel. If you want even more advice on gardening, from locating garden supplies to growing a perfect lawn, check out the full-size version of *Gardening Basics For Dummies* — simply head to your local bookseller or go to `www.dummies.com`!

Chapter 1

Playing the Name Game

In This Chapter

- Understanding how plants are named
- Identifying the parts of a plant

What's in a name? For gardeners, plenty. Gardening is a blend of horticulture and botany, common names and high science, and the names can get a bit confusing. Whether you're looking at plant anatomy or you simply want to know what to call a plant, understanding a bit about naming can help you wade through the aisles, ask better questions, and treat your plants right.

Hello, My Name Is . . . : Getting Used to Plant Nomenclature

Whenever you're talking about plants, knowing how they're named can help you avoid getting tangled up in the Latin. Generally, when looking for plants and flowers, you encounter two types of names — botanical and common. Read on for some info on how the naming system works, and then *carpe diem* — pluck the day!

Botanical names

The *botanical name* is the proper or scientific name of a plant. It consists of two parts: the genus name and the species name. The species name is kind of like your own first name (except it comes last in a plant's botanical name). The genus name is similar to your family name (except in botanical names, it comes first). For example, in the plant name *Hosta undulata, Hosta* is the genus name and *undulata* is the species name. *Hosta* describes an entire genus of famous, mostly shade-loving plants named hostas, and *undulata* describes the type of hosta it is — a hosta with an undulating leaf shape.

Sometimes the botanical name has a third name, right after the species name, known as the *variety.* A *variety* is a member of the same plant species but looks different enough to warrant its own name, such as *Rosa gallica var. officinalis.*

Still another botanical name that sometimes comes up is the *cultivar,* or cultivated variety. Cultivars are usually named by the people who developed or discovered them, and they're often maintained through cuttings, line-bred seed propagation, or tissue culture. In other words, they're cultivated (humans grow, improve, and develop them). An example is *Lychnis coronaria* 'Angel's Blush.'

A *hybrid* plant is the result of the cross-pollination between two genetically different plants, usually of the same species but different varieties. This combination can happen because of cultivation, or it can occur naturally through bee pollination between two different plants.

Botanical names are more common with some types of plants than others. For instance, you frequently run into them with herbaceous plants, trees, and shrubs but much less so with roses, annuals, and vegetables. You can find botanical names on the labels and in many garden references.

Common names

Common names are what you're most likely to encounter when shopping for plants to put in your garden, and they're what you mostly encounter in this book. You can find these names prominently displayed on seed packets or on seedling trays of plants that are for sale. They're kind of like botanical nicknames that gardeners use to describe a certain type of plant without going into a great amount of detail. For example, the *Hosta undulata* fits into the genus *Hosta,* so most gardeners merely refer to these plants under the common name of hostas. And you may know that *Hemerocallis* is actually the genus name for the common daylily, but chances are that most gardeners you encounter just call them daylilies.

Anatomy 101: Naming Plant Parts

Beyond recognizing the names of plants, knowing the various parts of plants is also useful. Figure 1-1 shows a nice, healthy perennial plant with the basic parts displayed. You probably already know most of them, but keep these parts in mind, because you need to know them to understand some of the things I discuss in the rest of this book! In the figure, the *taproot* is the main root of the plant; the *stolon,* or *runner,* is a horizontal stem that spreads through the ground to help some perennials propagate.

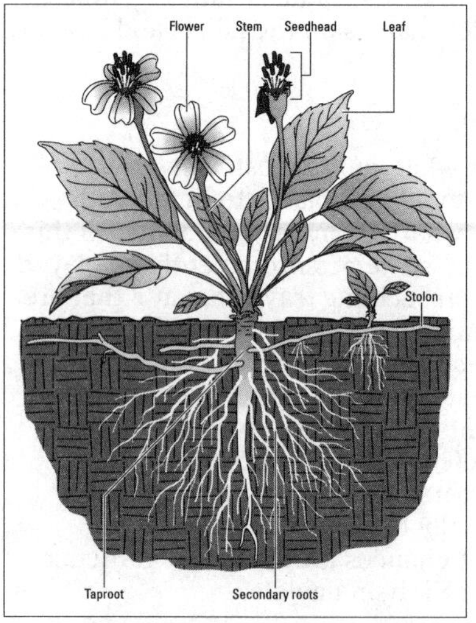

Figure 1-1: The basic parts of a perennial plant, above and below ground.

When you know the parts of plants and the differences among all the plant names you run into, you may be ready to get the lowdown on the types of plants out there!

Chapter 2

Live Long and Prosper: Giving Plants What They Need

In This Chapter

- Letting in enough light
- Figuring out fertilizer and mulch
- Getting the right amount of water

Time to get down and dirty! When you properly prepare the foundation of your garden, making sure plants can get what they need, success follows. The formula is as simple as that.

Well, maybe not. Is your soil in great condition? Do you have the right amount of soil nutrients and rainfall so your garden can thrive without any help from you? Not likely! For most people, improving the soil they have and taking charge of garden watering are necessities. This chapter tells you how to give plants a boost.

Improving a bed or area prior to planting is so much easier than doing so after. Do these tasks early if you can. If you can't, well then, at least make it a practice to dig really fabulous holes for each plant.

Let There Be Light!

Every plant needs at least some light in order to grow and prosper, but the amount really varies. Mushrooms, for instance, can grow in bins in a dim basement or shed; daisies and waterlilies, on the other hand, crave hot, full-on sunshine. Plenty of plants rest in the middle of these two extremes, of course. And some plants, like azaleas and daylilies, grow well enough in less-optimum light but don't flower well in the shade. In terms of labeling, just remember that *full sun* usually means six or more hours per day; *part-day,* of course, refers to less.

Leaves are the main "engine room" of a plant. For a plant to operate, thrive, and increase in size, all plant parts (except flowers) need to play their roles in photosynthesis. Roots draw in water, but the real energy production takes place primarily in the foliage. Light helps produce the fuel.

Long hours of plentiful sunlight, with varying angles throughout the day, are important so that every leaf — even the ones lower down on the plant — gets the chance to receive light. The good news is that no matter what light conditions your yard has to offer, at least something should be able to grow there.

The warmth of the sun, even more than actual light, inspires flowers to unfurl. Sunlight from the east (morning light) is considered cooler, and western sun (afternoon light) can be scorching. Many plants prefer a site with some morning sun, even until midday, and late-afternoon shade. Other plants are able to endure even the hottest conditions. A plant's tolerance, of course, varies by region. You can place the same plant in a sunnier spot in the far North than you can in the South.

If you have plants growing in a spot that receives a blast of late-afternoon sun, be sure to monitor their water needs closely so they don't dry out. If you find they're struggling, you can help them by installing something to cast a shadow, such as an arbor, or by planting a tree or large shrub in just the right spot. Even companion perennials or annuals planted nearby can cast enough shade to bring needed relief.

Here are some signs that a plant is getting too much sun:

- Flower petals dry out.
- Leaf edges look burnt or dried.
- Flower color looks faded or washed out.
- The entire plant starts to flag.

And here are signs that a plant isn't getting enough light:

- Growth is sparse.
- Stems are lanky and spindly.
- The distance between leaves, where they're attached to the stems, is especially wide.
- You see fewer flower buds and, thus, fewer flowers.
- The entire plant leans toward the light source.

Some of figuring out the proper location is trial and error: You're aware that roses like a full day of sun, but you really want that bush to go in the nook that gets afternoon shade. Give the spot a try. If the plant's unhappy, you can always move it to another spot.

Facing the Fertilizer Facts

Fertilizing (supplying your plants with supplemental minerals) is an important part of gardening. A well-timed dose of fertilizer really boosts a plant. You can't argue with success!

Just as a healthy diet allows a person or animal to prosper, so does a good and appropriate supply of nutrients keep a plant healthy and happy. The three primary plant-growth elements, or nutrients, are

- **Nitrogen (N):** Enhances stem and leaf growth. (For most plants, nitrogen ends up being the most important nutrient.)
- **Phosphorus (P):** Contributes to flower production, fruit production, seed production, and root growth.
- **Potassium (K):** Ensures general vigor; helps plants resist disease.

An all-purpose, balanced formulation contributes to overall plant health. These top three nutrients are usually listed on the back labels of bags of fertilizer that you can buy in any garden-supply store. They're usually listed in order as numbers on the package (N-P-K). A *balanced* fertilizer (one that contains the three most important elements — nitrogen, phosphorus, and potassium) may show up as 5-10-5 or even 5-10-10. Nitrogen-heavy lawn fertilizer usually has a high first number. You can find plenty of other variations, depending on the intended use of the fertilizer.

A fertilizer label often tells you which kind of fertilizer is best for your particular garden. If in doubt about your garden's exact needs, talk to someone at your local garden nursery or supply store.

Certain plants demand more or less of the top three nutrients (for instance, lawn grass loves nitrogen best). But most garden flowers are not specialists, which is why generally fertile soil is desirable and why all-purpose fertilizer is most commonly recommended.

Good soil also contains secondary nutrients, like calcium, magnesium, and sulfur, as well as some trace elements, called *micronutrients,* that enhance plant health and growth. You usually don't have to add these nutrients to the soil. However, soil tests sometimes indicate that gardeners should add micronutrients or secondary nutrients, especially calcium.

Fertilizing good soil is often optional. If you have fertile, organically rich soil, many of your plants may do just fine without it — particularly if you develop the habit of amending the soil regularly (once or twice a year) with more organic matter. If your garden soil is organically rich, it's fertile and, thus, should have the major elements. If not, or if you're pushing your plants to peak performance, you can use plant food or fertilizer to supply or supplement these important nutrients.

Constantly fertilizing lousy soil isn't a good idea. Not only is it a lot of work and expense for you, but it's also a losing battle. Salts build up, plants are never really healthy in the long term, and the soil texture remains poor. You're far better off increasing the organic matter and just using fertilizer as a nutrient boost for your plants — if they need it. *Organic matter* (once-living material that releases nutrients as it decays) includes compost, dehydrated manure, chopped leaves, damp peat moss, and ground-up bark.

Depending on what you use, how much, the plant in question, and so forth, the effects of adding fertilizer can be impressive. But they're not instant. Wait two weeks to a month before assessing the results.

You can't go wrong taking the time and effort to build up soil fertility and structure at least once a year, more often if the opportunity presents itself. Add it to every planting hole (except when planting trees and shrubs), sprinkle some on the soil surface at planting time, and deliver more over the root zone mid-season.

Much Ado about Mulch

Mulch is a good gardening habit but not mandatory. But, oh boy, do the benefits make it worth the effort! A really good job of mulching your garden usually

- Inhibits weed germination and growth
- Holds in soil moisture, protecting your plants from drying out so fast

- Moderates soil-temperature fluctuations
- In cold-winter areas, protects plant roots from winter cold and helps prevent *frost-heaving,* in which plants are literally pushed out of the ground by the natural expansion and contraction of the soil as it cools off and heats up
- In hot-summer areas, helps keep plant roots cooler
- Depending on what you use, adds a bit of welcome nutrition to your garden as it breaks down

Sound like good enough reasons to use mulch? Yeah, I thought I'd convince you. Read on for the lowdown.

Knowing your mulches

I can't name any "right" or "best" mulch. Benefits vary in different climates and parts of the country. Some mulches are free, right in your own backyard; you can purchase others locally. Experiment to find out what you and your plants prefer. Here are the pros and cons of some of the more popular options:

- **Grass clippings:** It's cheap, readily available, and easy to apply. On the downside, it decays quickly, so you have to replenish it often; if you use weed killers on your lawn or nitrogen-heavy fertilizer, it may adversely affect other parts of the garden; it can turn slimy if you apply more than an inch or so at a time; and if the grass went to seed before you cut it, the grass seeds can germinate in your garden beds.
- **Wood or bark chips:** It looks neat and attractive, stays where you put it, and is slow to decay. On the other hand, pine bark mulch is fairly acidic, which you may or may not want for your garden;

also, if you apply wood or bark chips too deeply (over 3 inches) or apply a deep layer against tree and shrub trunks, you may create a hiding spot for a bark-damaging rodent, especially in winter.

- **Decaying leaves:** They smother weeds very well and help hold in soil moisture. On the downside, they're not especially attractive; if they contain seeds, they can germinate and become a weed problem; if the leaves are soft, like maple leaves, the mulch can mat; and if they're acidic (oak especially), they can lower your garden soil's pH.
- **Compost:** It's free and plentiful if you have your own compost pile, and it adds nutrients to the soil as it breaks down. On the other hand, it makes a good place for weeds to take hold, and fresh compost (especially if it contains manure or grass clippings) can burn plants.
- **Peat moss:** It looks neat and tidy and is versatile — plus, it functions as a soil amendment. On the other hand, it can be expensive; if dry, it'll repel water; and it becomes crusty over time.
- **Gravel, pebbles, or stone:** It has a nice, neat look; it's easy to apply; it won't wash away easily and will last a long time; and it doesn't need to be replenished over the course of a season in colder climates. On the downside, it can allow weeds to sneak through and provides no benefits to the soil.
- **Plastic (garden plastic, black plastic):** Keeps weeds at bay and holds in soil moisture and warmth. On the other hand, watering and feeding is hard (you need to cut openings for plants), it can be difficult to apply unless you're doing an entire area at one time, and it isn't very attractive.

How to apply mulch — and how much

If you're ready to start applying mulch to your garden, here are some basic guidelines to ensure you get the best possible use of your mulch:

- **When you plant:** Applying mulch right after planting something is easy. Use a shovel or scoop with a trowel. Spread the mulch over the root-zone area but not flush up against a plant's base or main stem. Depth depends on the sort of plant. Annuals and perennials are fine with an inch or so of mulch; shrubs, roses, and trees need 3 or 4 inches or more.
- **During the growing season:** Add more mulch midway through the growing season or whenever you notice it's depleted. You may have to get down on your knees or wriggle around a bit as you try to deliver it where it's needed without harming the plant or its neighbors. Again, use less for smaller plants, more for bigger ones.
- **In the fall or for winter protection:** Depending on the severity of your winters and the amount of snow cover you expect (a blanket of snow can act as a protective mulch, actually), you want to cover an overwintering plant well. You can cut down perennials first and then practically bury them under several inches of mulch. You shouldn't trim back shrubs and rosebushes at this time, but you don't have to be as careful as you were with midsummer mulching because the plant is no longer growing actively. For freezing winters, 6 or more inches around the base of these is good.

To limit erosion, don't excavate large areas that are on a slope without planting or at least mulching soon, especially during the spring, when rainy weather can cause washouts.

Water, Water Everywhere: Tackling Watering Issues

Sure, without moisture, plants die. Everyone knows that. But you may not know why water is so incredibly vital. The answer is threefold, actually:

- Sufficient water pressure within plant tissues creates *turgor,* or rigidity, so the plant can stand up. A plant without turgor pressure collapses.
- Water keeps nutrients flowing through the soil, the roots, and the plant parts as they should.
- The plant uses light, carbon dioxide, and water to make sugar. Without photosynthesis, plants can't grow or develop flowers or fruit.

Keeping a close eye on your plants is easier said than done, of course, but the following sections tell you what you need to know, to keep in mind, and to watch out for when evaluating just how much moisture your garden needs.

Providing plants with the right amount of moisture

How do you make sure your garden has the right amount of moisture? Relying on natural rainfall would be nice, but natural rainfall is hard to count on (though it does kindly water your garden for you from time to time). Gardeners always seem to have to supplement the moisture, a little or a lot. You just need to keep an eye on things and pay attention to your plants. Read on for the warning signs of too much or too little water.

On the dry side

If you know what to look for, you can figure out your plants' watering needs. Plants actually prioritize when water-stressed, so look for the early warning signs: If a plant isn't getting enough water, flower petals and buds are the first things to be jettisoned (or fruit if it has developed), because making and maintaining them takes so much energy and water. Next to go are the leaves, which shrivel. Then the stems flop. Underground, the roots go limp. Obviously, if your garden is in this condition, it needs more water.

Bogged down

Telling when a plant doesn't have enough water may seem to be a snap, but keep in mind that there's definitely such a thing as too much water. If puddles form in your garden or an area of it is quite soggy, all the pores in the soil fill. When this happens, no free oxygen, which needs to get to the roots, is in the soil.

Meanwhile, some plant diseases (like mildew and blight) travel via water and can easily develop and spread in soaked conditions. Sodden roots blacken and rot, and all the aboveground growth subsequently dies. Garden plants in these circumstances, of course, need less water.

Unfortunately, an overwatered plant looks the same as one that's underwatered! The reason is that an overwatered plant is actually suffering from dehydration because the roots have been damaged by too much water (actually, too little oxygen, because the water has displaced the oxygen); the roots can't absorb water, so the plant wilts. One difference is that overwatered plants don't recover from wilt when you apply additional water, but underwatered ones generally do.

Determining which watering system to use

The amount of water your garden needs depends on what kind of soil you're using, what your climate is like, and what kinds of plants you have. Shallow-rooted plants, for example, need more water than deep-rooted ones for the simple reason that they're closer to the soil surface, which dries out more quickly in the heat of the sun. Deep roots can reach the more consistently damp lower soil layers.

For many gardeners, getting enough water to their gardens is the biggest gardening challenge. If you're crunched for time or have a large area to water, installing in-ground sprinklers and irrigation systems may be a good idea. Employing the use of a regular watering system, such as drip irrigation or an in-ground system, is the best approach to ensuring a consistent moisture cycle to grow happy, healthy plants. However, in-ground watering systems tend to be expensive and should be installed by professionals.

Of course, you can always water your garden yourself, by hand, and really that's a great way to do it, because you can personally inspect each plant.

Whether you water by hand or use a system, here are some things you may want to keep in mind:

- Watering your garden early in the morning, before the sun is fully overhead, is usually best. Watering at night can make plants susceptible to diseases that cause them to rot.
- Some plants in your garden, such as melons, may require more water than others, in which case watering by hand is probably best.
- If you don't have an outdoor spigot close to your garden for convenient hose hookup and watering, a rain barrel may be a good substitute for keeping water close to your garden. Various mail-order suppliers sell rain barrels.

  Warning: Make sure you get a barrel that's tall enough so pets can't get in, or put on covers to reduce drowning risks to pets and children. To keep mosquitoes out, use products like Mosquito Dunks, which are donuts of a type of bacteria that's harmless to humans but deadly to mosquito larvae.
- Usually, watering the soil rather than the leaves is best because the roots are what absorb water, and they're in the soil. Also, wetting the leaves can result in more disease problems. Still, on a very hot or windy day, watering the leaves can reduce wilt and lower leaf temperatures.
- Unless you have a very large garden, sprinkler heads that you attach to garden hoses are usually better suited for lawns than gardens. If you decide to use one, make sure the sprinkler covers the entire garden area evenly and doesn't water things you don't want watered, like your lawn furniture or windows.

- No matter what kind of garden you have or which watering system you use, infrequent deep soakings are better than frequent shallow waterings.

Cutting back on watering

Even if you don't live in an area experiencing drought, you don't want to waste water, no matter what you pay for it or how much you have to use. Remember that for most efficient delivery, water in early to mid-morning — after the dew has dried but before the heat of the day sets in and much of the water evaporates. And mulch, mulch, mulch individual plants and entire beds to hold in the water right by the roots, where plants most need and appreciate it. I go into more detail about mulch earlier in the chapter in "Much Ado about Mulch."

Wherever possible, build up a basin of mounded-up dirt or mulch around the edge of the rootball of each plant at planting time. Water goes right in the basin and soaks directly down into the root system instead of running off onto the lawn or driveway or elsewhere where it isn't needed.

The method of delivery can also save water: In-ground irrigation systems are wonderfully efficient; soaker hoses are also good. Drip systems shouldn't produce any appreciable runoff on slopes. And although some sprinklers are good, others are very wasteful. Check out mail-order catalogs that specialize in sprinklers; they're filled with good information on how to choose the right ones.

Depending on what kind of soil you have and how well it absorbs, you may find it worthwhile to run the water slowly rather than fast, and perhaps ten minutes on, ten minutes off — either or both of these techniques often drenches an area quite efficiently with little waste.

Rain gauges are useful for measuring water when you apply it with overhead sprinklers. For drip systems, run them for an hour or two and then dig down into the soil around the plant to see how far down and wide the moisture has penetrated. Run the system longer if it hasn't yet penetrated deep enough to reach the root zone. After you do this exercise a few times, you should know how long to run the system each time you water.

Another way to cut back on the amount of watering you need to do is to use drought-tolerant plants in your garden. Drought-tolerant plants include cacti, succulents, ceanothus, rock rose, native dryland plants and their cultivars (such as penstemon and gaura), and deep-rooted perennials like prairie natives and their cultivars (such as baptisia, liatris, black-eyed Susans, and purple coneflowers).

Chapter 3

Growing Annuals: Adding Yearly Variety to Your Garden

In This Chapter

- Identifying annuals
- Planting and caring for annuals

For sheer flower power, annuals are hard to beat. Because they have to complete their entire life cycle in one growing season — which is the technical definition of the term *annual* — these plants work fast. They go from seed or seedling to full-grown plant, bursting with flowers, in short order, delivering color when and where you need it. Gardening with annuals, more than ever, is easy and rewarding.

Finding Flowers That Fit Your Garden

Modern-day annuals are impressive indeed. They've been bred to produce abundant flowers and lush foliage throughout the heart of the growing season. They rush to flowering because their means of reproduction is by seed. And to get there, the flowers must come first. This great output guarantees bountiful garden color and also makes most annuals great for bouquets. By the time fall comes and seeds form (if they do, before frost), the plants are spent and die. By then, though, you should certainly have gotten your money's worth! Annuals are very gracious guests.

Not surprisingly, a huge range of annuals is on the market, and more annuals arrive every year. Demand is market-driven, innovation pushes on, and the upshot is that you can choose from many, many different annuals — no matter where you live, no matter what growing conditions your garden offers. The variety of annuals allows you to find countless plants that are specific to warm or cool weather.

Some like it hot: Warm-weather annuals

Lots of annuals thrive in hot summer weather. Many annuals have this preference because their predecessors, or ancestors if you will, originated in warm, tropical climates with long growing seasons. All plant breeders did was capitalize on or preserve these qualities while improving the plants' appearance or expanding the color range.

Some warm-weather annuals are actually perennial in some regions but are used as annuals in other areas because they're not hardy there — they don't survive the winter. For instance, snapdragon can be a perennial in the South but is used as an annual farther North. Some tropical plants are also commonly used for temporary display.

Examples of favorite warm-weather annuals include impatiens, Madagascar periwinkle, and marigolds.

Some annuals like it cool

Some annuals have their origins in areas with colder winters and mild but not blazingly hot summers. Plant breeders have stepped in to improve these plants' flower production (the more blooms, the merrier!), add new colors, and select for compact plant *habit* (shapes or forms). The result is a huge range of good, tough plants that even gardeners with shorter growing seasons can count on. Examples of favorite cool-weather annuals include cleome (spider flower), pansy, Johnny jump-ups (a type of viola), trailing lobelia, and calendula (pot marigolds).

North or South, cool-loving annuals are often a fine choice for the parts of your garden where shade prevails. The shelter of a fence, *pergola* (a type of arbor), porch, or overhanging tree keeps the plants cooler, preserving their flower color, prolonging bloom time, and protecting the plants from drying out in the hot sunshine.

Southern summers are generally too hot for cool-season annuals. Enjoy them until late spring and then tear them out as they begin to flag and replace them with something more durable.

An Annual Event: The Whens, Wheres, and Hows of Planting

Well, of course, in Northern gardens, annuals bloom in the summer months — and often, they start in spring and don't quit till fall. Lucky gardeners in milder areas with longer growing seasons can enjoy some annuals, especially those that are frost tolerant, year-round. Your growing conditions and climate dictate how soon the show gets started, how long it lasts, and where and how you should plant your annuals.

Filling in the garden after the last frost

If you live in an area with a long growing season, you can go ahead and sow annual seeds straight into the ground, secure in the knowledge that they'll sprout, grow up, and start pumping out flowers, all in plenty of time. This approach is generally easy and cheap. Gardeners with shorter summers can either start seeds inside or buy seedlings.

Freezing weather kills or at least severely damages most annuals. Therefore, the trick is to know your last spring frost date and your first fall frost date — these dates bookend the annual-gardening year. (If you don't know, ask an employee at a local garden center, a more experienced gardener, or someone at the nearest office of the Cooperative Extension service. Note that the dates are averages; they can vary somewhat from one year to the next.)

Planting in late spring

The majority of annuals are frost-sensitive. In other words, a freeze can damage or kill them. Frigid temperatures also make annuals much more susceptible to disease damage. If these small plants are damaged by cold, they may never quite recover. Don't risk it: Plant your new annuals in the ground only after all danger of frost is past.

Planting annuals later in the season

Of course you can plant later in the season! Plant and replant all summer long if you want and into fall if you garden in a mild climate. As long as the plants are willing and able to grow and produce flowers, why not?

Because blazing-hot weather is stressful, avoid planting during such spells or at least coddle the newcomers with plentiful water and some sheltering shade until they get established. A dose of all-purpose fertilizer (applied according to the instructions and rates on the container) may also hasten latecomers along.

Deciding where to plant annuals

By and large, annuals are resilient plants that tolerate a wide range of growing conditions. But some have preferences for more or less sun, and these specialists allow you to dress up such areas for maximum impact.

Planting in the sun

Full-on, warm sunshine inspires many annuals to grow robustly and generate loads of flowers. You can always tell if a sun-loving annual isn't getting enough light, because its stems become leggy and lean toward the light source, and flower production is disappointing. So let them have it! How much is enough? Six to eight hours a day suits most. My favorite annuals for sun include cosmos, nasturtiums, zinnias, marigolds, and cornflower.

Planting in the shade

Banish gloom in your yard's dim and tree-shaded areas with shade-loving annuals. Plenty do just fine in shade.

Indeed, their flowers last longer without the stress of the sun beating down on them. White and yellow flowers really add sparkle, individually or massed. My favorite annuals for shade include tuberous and fibrous begonias, impatiens, and torenia.

If your shade areas have poor soil or are laced with tree and shrub roots, don't despair. Instead, just display the plants in pots, setting them here and there or in clusters. Or dig holes in the ground and stick the plants — pots and all — in the hole. Doing so makes changing them out easy, too. (A clever idea: Hook hanging baskets over tree branches and fill them with shade-tolerant annuals.)

Getting annuals in the ground

Annuals are simple to plant. Just follow the label directions for spacing, and dig a hole deeper and wider than the root ball. Add some compost to the hole or mix the native soil with organic matter. If desired, you can add some dry fertilizer in the planting hole and water it in, or you can fertilize the annual after planting.

Annuals are most frequently sold in *market packs,* in which six or so plants are each in separate cells. Merely turn the pack upside down and gently push each plant out of its cell from the bottom. Don't pull them out from the top because the stem may break off from the roots. After removing the plants from the packet, plant them in the ground so that their rooting mass is slightly below the soil surface. Firm the soil around the plants and then water them in well.

Watering Your Annuals

Sufficient water is always important for growing plants, but even more so for productive annuals; consider it fuel for the ongoing show. Moisture hydrates the roots, plumps up the leaves, makes buds swell and open, and sustains the flowers. Don't allow your annuals to wilt before being revived or they'll be stressed out and unable to perform their best. Regular watering is ideal. Keep the following in mind when setting up a watering schedule for your annuals:

- **Spring watering:** If your area gets normal, drenching spring rainfall, your newly transplanted-into-the-garden annuals may not need supplemental water from you. But early watering encourages the roots to gain a foothold in their new home before the plant can properly turn its attention to growth and flowering. So water on day one and keep an eye on things in the ensuing days and weeks.
- **Summer watering:** Established annuals tend to be pretty tough and often forgive your watering lapses. But they'll certainly be healthier and look much better if you give them water at regular intervals and nurture them through periods of drought.
- **Fall watering:** In some areas, rainfall may take care of your annuals at this time of year. But if not, continue to water as needed so your annuals look terrific right up to the finish line (the first frost).

Your best watering methods depend on how many annuals you have and how close together they are. Options range from a gentle spray from a watering can to soaker hoses to a sprinkler. Watering in the morning hours is best so the water can soak in and hydrate the annuals through the hot midday.

Chapter 4

Growing Perennials: Plants That Make a Comeback

In This Chapter

- Examining perennials
- Putting plants in the ground for the long haul
- Keeping perennials happy

Perennials are flowering plants that are meant to last — several years, at least, and sometimes much longer. So ideally, they're a wise and practical "one-time investment," unlike the annuals you have to buy and replant every year; therein lies their great appeal and value. This chapter arms you with the basics so you can be a successful and happy perennial gardener!

Looking at Perennials, the Repeat Performers

The broadest definition of a *perennial plant* simply states that it's a *herbaceous,* or non-woody, plant — as opposed to, say, a shrub or tree — that lasts a couple years or more.

Perennials, like lilies and daffodils, can be bulbs. Herbaceous perennials are plants that have foliage that dies back to the ground, and new foliage and shoots sprout from their overwintering roots next spring.

Perennial plants are a wonderfully varied group, quite possibly the most varied group a gardener can work with. No matter where you live and what your growing conditions are (climate, soil type, sun or shade), you have plenty of plants to choose from. So which perennials should you include in your garden? Start off by knowing which general group can work best for you:

- **Hardy perennials:** The broad group of hardy perennials is justly popular in colder climates. These plants emerge each spring, producing foliage and flowers. Come fall, their top growth dies down and the show is over for the year. But the roots live on underground, waiting to revive and do it all again when warm weather returns. *Examples:* aster, columbine, coneflower, daylily, delphinium, mums, penstemon, peony, phlox, and Shasta daisy.
- **Tender perennials:** Contrary to popular belief, the upper parts of the Northern Hemisphere don't have the corner on perennials. Lots of plants from milder climes meet the perennial description. These repeat performers burst forth in warm spring weather, enjoy the summer months, and slow down or die down in the fall, roots still very much alive. They return in glory when the year cycles around to springtime again. *Examples:* angelonia, coleus, gerbera, impatiens, and pentas.

Planting Perennials

Perennials are probably the hottest topic these days among garden enthusiasts and plant suppliers. As a result, information about how to select and plant them abounds. Reputable garden centers have knowledgeable salespeople, and universities, garden centers, and public libraries sponsor various workshops and lecture programs about them. If you need more information than you find in the sections ahead, check out these sources and the books in your public library or local bookstore.

Figuring out where to plant perennials

Good news: There's a perennial for almost any growing situation your yard can dish up. Make a match between the conditions you have to offer and the known characteristics of a plant, and you're halfway there. A little care from you on planting day and beyond, and your perennials are sure to thrive.

Sunny locations

Lots of perennials adore sunshine. They grow more compactly when they get enough sun (as opposed to becoming lanky or leaning toward the light source), and they produce more and better flowers.

Full sun means six or more hours per day. If you have to choose between a spot with morning sun and a spot with afternoon sun, most sun-loving perennials seem to do better with the afternoon site. This situation varies somewhat depending on your climate. If you live in the deep South, a plant that grows best in full sun in a Northern climate may perform better in a spot protected from hot, late-afternoon sun.

Because sun can be drying, either choose dryland natives or help out the plants with regular watering and a moisture-conserving mulch around their root systems.

Favorite sun perennials include artemisia, armeria, basket-of-gold, blanket flower, coneflower, coreopsis, delphinium, gaura, lavender, penstemon, peony, sea holly, and yarrow.

Shady spots

Judging from many gardening books and magazines, a beautiful garden is full of sunshine and flowers, and those of us with shade are doomed to a dull and boring display. Not so! Many perennials prefer shade, prospering in a range of conditions ranging from deepest woodland gloom to areas of dappled or filtered light to those that get morning sun and afternoon shade.

Not only that, but many plants appropriate for shade have beautiful leaves — you can find amazing variety in shape, texture, and even color. And you may be pleasantly surprised to hear that plenty of shade plants produce attractive flowers.

Shade is actually a benefit to many plants. Lack of direct sun means their leaves look healthy and lush, without burned edges or tips, without drying out or wilting. Sunlight also tends to bleach out the beauty of *variegated leaves* (leaves that are marked or rimmed in white, cream, or gold), whereas in shade, such foliage thrives and lights up the scene. Shelter from the sun's hot rays also preserves flower color.

Favorite shade perennials include ajuga, astilbe, bergenia, bleeding heart, brunnera, coral bells, corydalis, many ferns, goatsbeard, hellebore, hosta, lady's mantle, lamium, lily-of-the-valley, lungwort, Solomon's seal, and sweet woodruff.

Dry soil

If sandy, gritty, or fast-draining soil is your lot, a fabulous perennial garden is still possible. Save yourself a lot of blood, sweat, and tears by working with what you have. Sure, digging in some organic matter at planting time (and on an annual basis) is good advice that you should follow when you can, but your gardening life can be a lot easier if you go native. You don't have to pour on water you don't have, and you may be delighted with the easy maintenance and attractive look.

That's right: Go native. Perennials native to dry ground are your best bet. Before you protest that they aren't attractive or are probably weeds, take a fresh look. Peruse the offerings at a local nursery that specializes in indigenous plants. Visit a public garden or botanic garden with displays of natives. Your eyes will be opened. Botanists and horticulturists feel your pain and have been working hard over the years to find out which ones adapt best to gardens and which ones are prettiest. There are even selections of cultivated varieties (cultivars) that are significant improvements over their wild parents — new flower colors and bigger, longer-lasting flowers on more-compact, handsome plants.

Favorite dry-soil perennials include black-eyed Susan, blanket flower, baptisia, butterflyweed, evening primrose, gaura, penstemon, phormium (a tender perennial in most regions), and yarrow. And don't overlook cacti and succulents — a well-stocked local or mail-order nursery can convince you of their astounding range and beauty.

Wet soil

Soggy, boggy ground is usually written off as a lost area or liability. But what if that damp side yard, wet back 40, or perpetually muddy roadside ditch were to come alive with handsome leaves and blooming color? It's certainly possible. A host of plants actually like wet feet; a little research can point you to the ones that are a match for your problem spot's conditions.

You may have to wade in prior to planting and get the spot ready. Bring your rubber boots and create a hospitable open area with gusto and determination! Yank out most or all of the existing vegetation so it doesn't compete with the desirable incoming perennials. If warranted and practical, dig a drainage trench to route excess water away from the spot. Perhaps dig in some organic matter to improve soil fertility and drainage, if only a little.

After you've planted the area with appropriate moisture-loving perennials, not much more should be required. The plants' basic need — water — is already present. If the plants are happy, they'll increase over time, reducing the need for weeding or indeed, any intervention on your part. If they grow too lushly, you can rip out and discard or give away the extra plants.

Cardinal flower, daylilies, forget-me-not, Japanese primrose, marsh marigold, and turtlehead are good plants for wet soil. Don't apologize for the wet soil: Go ahead, call it a bog garden! And if you're ambitious, make the boggy area the entry to a new water garden.

Clay soil: Soggy soil at its worst

If your yard has clay soil, you already know it. Slick and soggy in wet weather and nearly impenetrable in dry, clay soil is actually composed of lots of densely packed, very tiny particles. Clay leaves little space for air and water to circulate, and the result is heavy ground that drains poorly. Needless to say, many perennials — or rather, their roots — have a hard go of it in such conditions (and so does your shovel or trowel, for that matter).

Clay soil does have some advantages, believe it or not. It's often fairly fertile because it holds nutrients and water so well. And, of course, it's slower to dry out in hot weather, which can help your plants.

At any rate, if clay is your lot in life, you have three options:

- **Improve the soil's structure by adding organic matter.**
- **Go with what you have.** Plant clay-tolerant perennials, such as beebalm, cardinal flower, chrysogonum, epimedium, many ferns, galax, gunnera, Japanese iris, Japanese primrose, marsh marigold, or myosotis.
- **Bypass it.** Grow your perennials in raised beds or pots.

Deciding when to plant perennials

Perennials tend to be rather tough and forgiving plants in terms of picking the right time to plant them, but most people plant perennials in either the spring or the fall.

Perhaps the best way to know when to plant perennials is to know when *not* to plant them. No-no times include

- Any blazing hot day
- Any time of drought
- Any time when frost is predicted
- Any time when the ground is soggy or still frozen
- Right after a heavy storm or flood

Read on for some seasonal planting advice.

Spring planting

Springtime is the preferred time to plant perennials for good reason. All the conditions these plants relish and respond to are in place: warming soil, warm sunshine, longer days, moist ground, and regular rainfall. Roots quest into the ground, taking up water and nutrients to fuel growth, and *top growth* (foliage, stems, and flowers) surges forth.

When getting ready for spring planting, make sure you do the following:

1. **Harden the plants off.**

   Let new plants adjust to life outdoors for a few days or a week by sitting them in a sheltered spot, such as on the porch or against the semi-shady side of the house. Start the plants off for just a few hours, and increase the time until they're outdoors 24/7. (But bring perennials indoors or cover them if there's a threat of a late frost.) Cover them with a single layer of newspaper to reduce the light intensity and wind exposure.

2. **Choose a cool, cloudy, or damp day to plant, or plant in late afternoon.**
3. **Plant in good soil, create a basin of soil or mulch around each plant, and give a good, soaking watering.**

   Check that the water drains in where you want it.
4. **Mulch after planting.**

Here are some things perennials find very unpleasant. During spring planting, do not

- **Handle the plants roughly.**
- **Plunk a root-bound plant into the ground.** Either tease apart the roots a bit or lightly score the sides with a sharp knife, which inspires new root growth. *Then* place the perennial in its hole.
- **Plant perennials in waterlogged ground, or drench them right after planting.** A moderate dose of water is a needed drink; too much water prohibits oxygen from getting to the roots, and the plants literally drown or rot.

Fall planting

Autumn turns out to be a fine time to plant many perennials in temperate climates. The soil and air are cooler now and sunlight is less intense, so the weather's less stressful for newcomer plants. Competition from weeds isn't likely to be a big problem, either.

In some regions, rainfall becomes more regular, too, which helps provide the moisture the perennials need to start good root growth. And their roots *do* grow — the plants simply aren't programmed to start producing lots of new leaves or flowers at this time of year.

Yes, the perennials will soon head into winter dormancy, but fall planting often gives these perennials a head start over their spring-planted counterparts.

Fall planting also applies to perennials you want to dig up and move to a new spot and to *divisions* (strong, rooted pieces of overgrown plants).

When getting ready for fall planting, make sure you do the following:

- Buy good, strong plants. They have the best chance to establish themselves in your garden.
- Mulch a little at planting time, about ½ to 1 inch, to hold in soil moisture and warmth; mulch even more as winter arrives, another 2 or 3 inches after the ground freezes, to protect the plants during the cold months. (For more info on mulching options, see Chapter 2.)
- Cut back the top growth, just to further urge the plant to concentrate on root growth.

Here are some things to *avoid* during fall planting:

- **Fertilizing:** Fertilizing inspires a fresh spurt of young shoots and leaves, which are vulnerable to cold damage. You want perennials to enter their winter dormancy.
- **Planting late-bloomers:** Late bloomers (like asters, mums, black-eyed Susan, and perennial ornamental grasses) are better planted in spring.

Make doubly sure, before you find out the hard way, which plants relish fall planting and which do not. You can always double-check at wherever you buy perennials in the fall.

Reputable nurseries don't sell plants that resent being planted this time of year. Some fall-planting favorites are daylilies, peonies, oriental poppies, and rhizomatous iris.

Show the Love: Taking Care of Your Perennials

Generally, perennials require the same type of care as annuals (see Chapter 3) with a few modifications that depend on the type and size of your perennials. Here I give you advice on how to handle basic perennial care issues.

Supporting with stakes or rings

Because some perennials are tall, or tall and broad, a little support is a good thing. It not only keeps the plant more in bounds and manageable, but it also prevents the plant from keeling over under its own weight. You've been waiting for those flowers — don't let them cast downward or flop on the ground!

Using a stouter or larger support than you think you need never hurts — if your perennials are healthy and happy, they're probably going to need it.

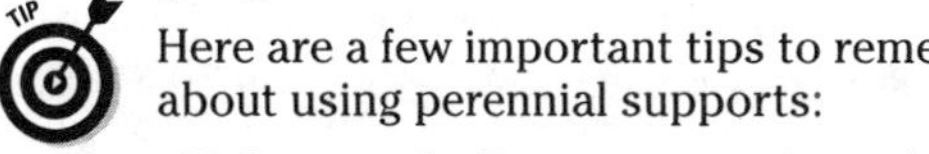

Here are a few important tips to remember about using perennial supports:

- **Install them early.** Press a *peony hoop* (a ring on legs that's useful for many more perennials than just peonies) over the plant well before it reaches the hoop's height. This way, you can center the support right over the plant, and when the perennial does grow as expected, the stems, leaves, and flowers will froth over the hoop and hide it from view — without a struggle. Early installation also reduces the risk of damaging the root system as you poke the support in.

- **Press the support in deeply.** At first, the support may be equal to the job, but as the plant grows ever larger, the stake or hoop may lean or slump. Anchoring the support deeply at the outset can make the support more stable and stronger. A foot or more into the ground is usually best, depending on the plant.
- **Help out with ties.** As the plant grows, check on it and fasten the stem or stems to the support at regular intervals. To avoid abrading the plant tissue, use soft material, not wire (try string or cloth); if you loop it once around the stem and create a second loop for attaching to the support, the plant will be able to move in a breeze but still be held gently but firmly to its appointed place. (Use green string or cloth, and you'll hardly be able to see it.)
- **Be tidy!** Remove and store or discard the support at season's end. This step will also remind you to cut back the perennial (and mulch if your winters are cold). With a season's experience under your belt, you should now know whether the support is the right one for the job and, thus, worth saving or replacing. If you need something more substantial, add it to your springtime shopping list.

You really don't know whether a perennial needs support until you grow it. Whether a support is necessary depends not only on the type of plant but also on cultural conditions — a plant that may be self supporting in full sun in a protected location may need to be staked if grown in a shady spot or one with a lot of wind. Perennials that do need support need it every year.

Preparing perennials for winter

If you live in a cold area and want to overwinter your tender perennials, simply dig up the roots or the entire plant and bring it indoors to a nonfreezing spot to spend a few months as a dormant or semi-dormant houseplant. Pot the plants in any good soil and grow them in a cool (40°F–50°F) and bright area. Keep them barely moist. The idea here is to just keep them alive until you can plant them back outside after the danger of frost next spring. Then, with warmer temperatures and brighter light, they'll spring back to life.

You can also trim and prune back your perennials and use mulch to protect them through the winter (see Chapter 2).

Chapter 5

Food, Glorious Food! Growing Your Own Veggies

In This Chapter

- Looking at veggies and vegetable-garden fruits
- Preparing your bed, sowing seeds, and planting

For the cost of a packet of seeds, you can have your own, homegrown produce. The requirements are simple: good soil, moisture, and full sun. This type of gardening is usually called vegetable gardening, even though it also involves growing items that are technically fruit, such as tomatoes and melons. Growing your own produce — or vegetables, as it were — can be fun and fairly easy for the beginner gardener. This chapter gives you the basics.

Varieties of Veggies

Vegetable varieties vary in many ways. That's what makes vegetable gardening possible for everyone and keeps it so interesting. You could garden all your life and still not get around to growing all the tempting choices that would prosper in your particular region!

Growing vegetables by seasons

Typically, the vegetable-gardening season is summer, bookended by late spring and early fall. Gardeners mark the start by the last spring frost date and the finish by the first fall frost date (although some crops, like parsnips and kale, can stay out in the cold a bit longer and even gain improved flavor).

Your local weather forecaster may announce the frost date each spring (last frost) and fall (first frost), or you can call your local garden center or the nearest Cooperative Extension office and ask. The dates vary somewhat from one year to the next.

Here's an overview of which vegetables tend to do better during which seasons:

- **Cool-season vegetables:** These plants tolerate some frost and temperatures between 55°F and 70°F. As such, they're fine choices for gardeners in more northern areas or, in milder climates, for growing in a cool spring or fall. *Examples:* asparagus, beets, broccoli, Brussels sprouts, cabbage, carrot, cauliflower, collard, endive, kale, kohlrabi, lettuce, onion, oriental greens, parsnip, peas, potato, radish, Swiss chard, spinach, turnip, and turnip greens.
- **Warm-season vegetables:** These plants are readily harmed by frost; they also fare poorly in cold soil. Grow these plants in temperatures ranging from 65°F to 80°F. They're good in the South and West and elsewhere during the height of summer. *Examples:* beans, corn, cucumber, eggplant, melons (watermelon, muskmelon/cantaloupe), pepper, sweet potato, pumpkin, squash, sweet corn, and tomato.

- **Perennials:** These edible plants live from one year to the next, typically producing good crops their second or third seasons and thereafter. You can grow them in most climates, providing a protective winter mulch if warranted. *Examples:* asparagus and rhubarb.

Working with the sun: Where to plant vegetables

Most fruiting vegetables like the environment sunny and open — the soil is warm, light is plentiful, and they grow easily, developing and ripening their fruit with minimal stress or impediments. (If conditions are not ideal, they make less fruit and take longer to ripen — also, the plants may lean or grow toward the light source in a bid to get as much as they can.) Examples of sun-loving vegetables include tomatoes, peppers, squash, beans, okra, eggplant, and corn.

To maximize needed sun, site your vegetable garden in a south-facing spot; plant taller plants to the north end so they don't cast shade over their shorter fellows.

Some vegetables are less dependent on full sun, which can fade or dry out their foliage or slow their growth. Or the plants may just like cooler temperatures. Vegetables that gardeners grow for their leaves fall into this group, as do ones with edible roots. Examples include lettuce, mixed greens (mesclun), chard, potatoes, carrots, and turnips.

To maximize sheltering shade, grow these vegetables in an east- or west-facing garden; site taller plants and objects (including trellises, teepees, and caged or staked tomatoes) in front of and to the south of these shade-lovers. Or grow these plants earlier in spring or in the fall — assuming you have enough time to ripen them before winter comes, that is.

Prepping your soil

The biggest mistake beginning vegetable gardeners make is using lousy or too-thin soil. Before a single vegetable begins its hopeful, potential-filled life in your yard, give it a very good home! This prep work can save you untold disappointment and, perhaps more than any other factor, assure a bountiful and delicious harvest.

If you're working with a brand-new vegetable garden (or one that fell fallow and you're bringing it back to life), stake it out and get it ready the autumn before you plan to plant. If a fall start isn't possible or practical, go ahead and prepare the ground in spring — but don't start too early.

How do you tell whether it's ready to be worked in? Grab a handful and squeeze — it should fall apart, not form a mud ball.

Follow these tips when preparing your soil:

- **Dig deep.** Most vegetables are content with 6 to 8 inches of good ground for their roots to grow in. If you're planning to grow substantial root crops (potatoes, say, or carrots), go deeper still — up to a foot or more.
- **Add lots and lots of organic matter.** Try compost, dehydrated cow manure, shredded leaves, well-rotted horse manure (call nearby stables), or a mixture thereof. Mix it with the native soil, 50-50, or even more liberally.

Planting Your Vegetables

You can start cool-season vegetables earlier than warm-season vegetables and put them in the ground earlier because they're more tolerant of cooler temperatures; some can even go outdoors before the last frost. Put warm-season vegetables out or sow them only after all danger of frost is past.

Deciding when to plant your veggies

Determining the date of the last frost is your green-light date, the date when you're now free to plant vegetable seedlings or direct-sow vegetable seeds into the garden. The last frost date is in late spring, but the date varies from year to year. You can find out down at the local garden center or from the nearest office of the Cooperative Extension Service.

When to plant transplants

If you have seedlings ready to go into the garden after the soil is ready and sufficiently warmed up — seedlings of your own or ones you've bought — your garden can get off to an earlier start. Vegetables that you can start early indoors include cabbage, tomatoes, peppers, and eggplant. On the other hand, if you start too early, your seedlings may be too big too early, making them a little hard to accommodate and care for — you may even have to start over.

Here's a general list to get you started; you can tinker as you get more experience raising various sorts of seeds:

- **Onions:** 4 to 6 weeks before the last frost
- **Broccoli, collards, and cabbage:** 5 to 6 weeks before the safe planting-out date (which is after the danger of snow and ice is past but while nights are still chilly)
- **Lettuce:** 4 to 5 weeks before the last frost
- **Peppers:** 8 to 12 weeks before the last frost
- **Tomatoes and eggplant:** 6 to 8 weeks before the last frost
- **Cucumbers and melons:** 2 to 4 weeks before the last frost

When to sow seeds directly

Gardeners generally sow seeds directly in the garden after the last frost, after the soil has warmed up and the weather seems to have settled into an early-summer groove. Direct-sowing in cold and/or soggy soil is a bad idea — it's muddy work for you, and the seeds usually sprout poorly or rot; then you have to start over.

Vegetables that you can direct-sow include lettuce, onions, peas, radishes, turnips, beets, cabbage, carrots, beans, corn, parsnips, cucumber, lettuce, and tomatoes (in warm climates).

Sowing and planting your veggies

How to plant vegetables really depends on the form in which you've acquired them. Do you want to plant seeds, or do you want to plant transplants that you've acquired? Or do you want to combine both approaches and create your own transplants from seeds? Here I give you information on all three approaches.

Starting your own seeds indoors

A sure way to banish the winter blues, as well as get a jumpstart on your vegetable garden, is to start some seeds indoors early. To find out how early, consult the back of the seed packet; you want to time it so you have several-inch-high seedlings in late spring, after the danger of frost in your area has passed. Refer to Figure 5-1 and follow these steps:

1. **Select a good spot.**

   In milder climates, gardeners can sow seeds early in a cold frame or greenhouse, if they have one. Everyone else has to make do indoors.

2. **Provide light.**

   Some seeds germinate under a thin layer of soil mix and some are pressed lightly on top, but in all cases, the seedlings that sprout need between 12 and 16 hours of light per day — that's a lot.

   To make your seedlings work, you need artificial light. Fluorescent is best; a timer at the outlet can help you regulate the hours it's shining on your baby plants.

3. **Prepare pots or flats (which need drainage holes).**

   Begin with sterile seed-starting mix. (This mix is available in bags wherever gardening supplies are sold. It looks like very fine potting mix.) Fill the containers about three-quarters full with dampened, not drenched, mix (see Figure 5-1A). Tamp the surface flat and level with the flat of your hand or a small piece of wood before sowing.

4. **Sow, following the instructions on the packet.**

   Sow carefully by hand — a pencil tip is a useful tool when placing small seeds (see Figure 5-1B). Don't sow too many seeds! This overplanting can lead to a forest of seedlings, growing too thickly for you to thin them without damaging some. If you're sowing into a flat, make little furrows with the pencil tip or a finger and space the seeds up to an inch apart (see Figure 5-1C).

5. **Cover the container the very day you plant.**

   Plastic wrap is great, but depending on the size of your starting containers, you can instead use a plastic bag (see Figure 5-1D). Don't seal too tightly, though. A tight seal causes condensed water to drip back down into the mix, making things too soggy.

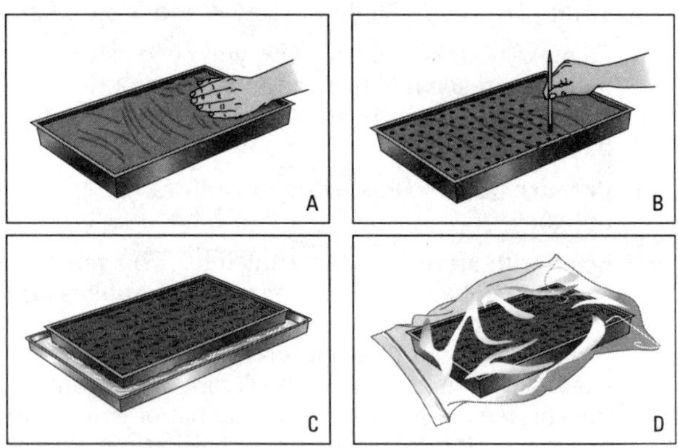

Figure 5-1: Seed-starting trays.

6. **Check back daily.**

   Don't let the planting mix dry out, or the seeds' growth will come to a halt. Open the bag a couple hours every few days to let the soil breathe some fresh air. Then close it back up. The best way to keep developing seedlings evenly and consistently moist is with bottom watering. Just set the container into a few inches of water (in the sink or a tray) and let it wick up the water it needs before returning the container to its spot.

Planting transplants in the garden

Regardless of whether you grow your transplants yourself or purchase them from a supplier, the first step toward getting them into the ground is the hardening-off process. This interim step in the life of your precious baby seedlings is a way to ease them from their plush indoor life to the realities of life in the real world — outdoors in the garden.

After the threat of frost has passed, move your seedlings outside to a place that's sheltered from sun and wind. Start with an hour a day, and gradually work it up to 24 hours over a two-week period. Stop fertilizing them.

When the seedlings are hardened off, you're ready to get the seedlings off to a good start. Ideally, work on an overcast day (or plant late in the day) when the hot sun won't stress them or you. Here's what to do:

1. **Water the seedlings well the morning you plan to plant.**
2. **Dig individual holes.**

The holes should be at least as deep and wide as the pot the seedling comes in. The tag that comes with the plant should tell you how much room to allow, but when in doubt, allow more elbow room rather than less.

3. **Pop each plant out of its pot carefully, handling the seedlings by gently gripping the leaves.**

   Tease apart the roots on the sides and bottom so they'll be more inclined to enter the surrounding soil in their new home. Place the roots gently in their hole and tamp the soil in around them firmly to eliminate air pockets.

4. **Water; then mulch.**

   Gently soak each seedling quite well, using a wand attachment on your hose or a watering can. Then lay down an inch or two of mulch an inch out from the base of each seedling and outward to conserve soil moisture as well as to thwart sprouting weeds. Don't let the mulch touch the stem, or you risk insect and pest problems later on.

Offer a little protection. Get them through the first few days by setting some boxes or boards nearby to create a barrier — or set a few lawn chairs out in the garden over the seedlings.

Sowing seeds directly into the garden

All danger of frost is past, the air and soil have warmed up, and the ground is slightly damp or even somewhat dry. In other words, it's very late spring or early summer, and you're ready to sow your seeds.

Assuming that the garden area is prepared and ready to go, head outdoors one fine day with seed packets, a trowel, a planting dibble or hoe, and something to sit on. Don't rush — putting seeds in this good Earth is a wonderful, soothing, productive feeling!

Follow these steps:

1. **Make planting holes or furrows.**
2. **Follow the "three friends" rule — plant three seeds per hole.**

   At least one will likely sprout well. If all three do, you can thin out two of them later to favor the most robust one.
3. **Cover each hole as you go, tamping down the soil to eliminate air pockets.**
4. **Label.**
5. **Water well with a soft spray so you don't dislodge the seeds.**
6. **Mulch (see Chapter 2).**

Spanish
DUMMIES
A Reference for the Rest of Us!
Spanish Phrases
DUMMIES
Baby Signing
DUMMIES
A Reference for the Rest of Us!

Baby & Toddler Meals
DUMMIES
A Reference for the Rest of Us!

Organizing
DUMMIES
A Reference for the Rest of Us!

Wedding Planning
DUMMIES
A Reference for the Rest of Us!

Healthy Aging
DUMMIES
A Reference for the Rest of Us!

Brain Games
DUMMIES

Improving Your Memory
DUMMIES
A Reference for the Rest of Us!

Su Doku
DUMMIES

With more than 1,400 titles to choose from, we've got a Dummies book for wherever you are in life!

Business/Personal Finance & Investment

Title	ISBN	Price
High-Powered Investing All-in-One For Dummies	9780470186268	$29.99
Investing For Dummies, 5th Edition	9780470289655	$21.99
Living Well in a Down Economy For Dummies	9780470401170	$14.99
Managing Your Money All-in-One For Dummies	9780470345467	$29.99
Personal Finance Workbook For Dummies	9780470099339	$19.99
Taxes 2009 For Dummies (January 2009)	9780470249512	$17.99

Crafts & Hobbies

Title	ISBN	Price
California Wine For Dummies (May 2009)	9780470376072	$16.99
Canning & Preserving For Dummies	9780764524714	$16.99
Jewelry & Beading Designs For Dummies	9780470291122	$19.99
Knitting For Dummies, 2nd Edition	9780470287477	$21.99
Quilting For Dummies, 2nd Edition	9780764597992	$21.99
Watercolor Painting For Dummies	9780470182314	$24.99

Fitness & Diet

Title	ISBN	Price
Dieting For Dummies, 2nd Edition	9780764541490	$21.99
Low-Calorie Dieting For Dummies	9780764599057	$21.99
Nutrition For Dummies, 4th Edition	9780471798682	$21.99
Exercise Balls For Dummies	9780764556234	$21.99
Fitness For Dummies, 3rd Edition	9780764578519	$21.99
Stretching For Dummies	9780470067413	$16.99